AF120377

ELEMENTS
and
EMOTIONS

DOROTHY CARTER

Elements and Emotions
Copyright © 2022 by Dorothy Carter

All rights reserved. No part of this publication may be reproduced, distributed, or transmitted in any form or by any means, including photocopying, recording, or other electronic or mechanical methods, without the prior written permission of the publisher, except in the case brief quotations embodied in critical reviews and other noncommercial uses permitted by copyright law.

ISBN: (Paperback)   978-1-63945-354-2
       (Hardcover)   978-1-63945-355-9
       (E-book)   978-1-63945-356-6

The views expressed in this book are solely those of the author and do not necessarily reflect the views of the publisher, and the publisher hereby disclaims any responsibility for them.

Writers' Branding
1800-608-6550
www.writersbranding.com
orders@writersbranding.com

Contents

Chapter One 1

Chapter Two 9

Chapter Three 19

Chapter Four 27

Chapter Five 37

Chapter Six 49

Chapter Seven 61

Chapter Eight 79

Chapter Nine 93

Chapter Ten... 105

Chapter Eleven 123

Chapter Twelve 137

Introduction

My poems are written to inspire and encourage you to read the bible for yourself, to learn of God, to know the truth about how he wants us to live our life. It is designed to let you know that we will all experience joy, sorrow, disappointment, and pain at one time or another. I implore you to hold on to your faith in God and appreciate the beauty of nature that he has made. The bible is the most important book ever written, it is a guide to how God wants us to worship and serve him as we live out our lives each day.

Dedications

I give honor to God, first and foremost; who is the beginning and the end of all things. To all my family, friends, and neighbors. A special thanks to my Daughter, Nedria Davis, for helping me put it all together. I would like to thank Mrs. Annette Murray Williams for her financial help in creating this book. To all my church family for supporting me through encouragement and prayer. To all those who love reading books of all forms and types. I pray you will enjoy my collection.

Foreword

This is my second book, and I pray that God will give me the inspiration to do more. I have been writing poetry since I was fifteen years old; at that time, they served a different goal. Writing gave me a sense of release from all my teenage problems, and I would find peace of mind. As the years went by, I came to know Christ, and he gave me a new focus on life. No matter what I was doing at a particular time, God would put a poem in my mind. He gave me the inspiration and the words to put down; so that whoever is lost, through these words, may be found. I can only do it with the help of God and by his will only.

CHAPTER ONE

The Seasons Of Age

From birth to twelve is the spring of age; thirteen to nineteen is the summer of hormonal rage. Autumn is the age we should fully mature; with so many responsibilities we try to endure. When the winter of our years has finally set in, we are grounded, confident, and on God we depend.

It's Not About You

Whatever you do for others, do with a loving heart; doing it for recognition is not pleasing to God. If you look for men to pat you on the back; all of your good deeds would just have been an act. If you seek to be put on a pedestal while here on earth; you are looking for men to validate your worth. God knows all that you do, and if your actions are really true. You will get your reward from above, if the things you do are done in brotherly love; so look for God's acceptance, and not that of men; your rewards will be waiting in heaven when he comes back again.

Idle Minds

When our minds are Idle, and there are things we want to do, Satan will creep in, and try to influence you; instead of patiently waiting, our minds begin debating. We think of ways we can make things happen, and come up with all kinds of reasons for our actions. We want things in our own time, instead of waiting for God to give us a sign. If we wait on God; we won't resort to evil deeds, because he has promised to supply all of our needs.

Nothing Hidden

Nothing in your mind or actions are hidden from God; he knows the thoughts of every heart. We may not know what's going on in your mind, but God knows at all times. Every act that you carry out, was conceived in your mind before it came about. Whether it was right or wrong; God knew it all along. Nothing is hidden, because God always knows the plan you have before it grows. Every wrong that you may do, will cause a consequence brought against you. Every kindness, and every good work, shines a light on your spiritual rebirth. Nothing is hidden, all is laid bare; you can't hide from God, because he's always there. If you want to enter into his place of rest; you must surely pass the test.

Guided By The Spirit

Why is it so easy for us to believe in the things that are designed just to deceive; instead of asking God to guide our thought process; we always think that we know what's best. When we lose the peace of mind that we once had, our conscious will stop us from going down the wrong path. If we are led by the Spirit of God; we will know what is right when he speaks to our hearts.

Battle Up Above

I see a blue sky peeking through the clouds, as if to make a statement and saying it out loud. It slowly pushes the clouds away; so it can cover the remainder of the day. The clouds are pushing back, as if to say; it's not that easy to drive me away. Blue skies, and clouds are in a tug of war, one must concede so the other can soar. Blue skies and clouds are about to converge, but only one will finally emerge.

Unsteady Faith

If you are constantly living with fear, and worried about what's going to happen today, tomorrow, or next year; our freedom to live our lives are rapidly passing us by, so do not focus on the what, when, or why. God is in control and worry is not helping you; whatever happens, there is nothing you can do. We cannot change what God allows; his will is supreme, and we all must bow. He can bring peace to our troubled mind, with an assurance that he will work things out in time.

Random Thought

The things we covet will not last; when we veer from God's chosen path. Random thoughts often cross our mind, of things we could have done differently at a particulier time. All the what if's, or if only I's; does no good to wonder why. We must live our lives according to God's design; not by keeping up with others and letting sin cloud our minds. We can't go back and change the things we have done, but we can pray for forgiveness from God, the most holy one.

Thanks For It All

Jesus Christ, the only son; through whom all our victories are won. The stars that light up the sky at night; sun that brings on another daylight. Trees and flowers that filter the air, providing fresh oxygen through your love and care. Food and water that keep us from despair; sustaining our bodies, because of your presence there. Being able to feel the rain on our face; the winter cold, and harsh embrace. Every step that we take,everyday that we awake. Our mind and body being as well as it is; so much to be thankful for each day that we live. Thank you God for it all; the things that are great, and the things that are small. For all the blessings that you freely give; we can't thank you enough for this life we live.

To And Fro

Satan is going to and fro; destroying relationships wherever he go; wreaking havoc whenever he can, trying to destroy the souls of man. He has become very bold; changing the hearts of men from the days of old. Turning them away from the God who died, and getting them to follow along his side. To and fro, he must make haste; his time is limited, he has no time to waste. He must win over the souls of men, to influence them to turn back to sin. There are so many souls to try and win; before his time comes to an end. He knows that God has so many that are strong, and won't be tempted to do what is wrong. God is in control without a doubt; when he gets ready, he will take Satan out.

CHAPTER TWO

Dust To Dust

God created us from the dirt; layered us with skin for our natural birth. We can wash our bodies with extra care, but the dirt in us will always be there. If you rub your skin hard enough, dirt beads will form and show up. It has nothing to do with the color of our face; we are all created by God's grace. Our bodies are made up of dirt, and will one day return back to the earth.

God Is In Control

When we lose a friend or loved one to sickness, accident, or in a violent way: we choose to blame God and turn ourselves astray. We ask God why? Why did you let my friend or relative die? It's so hard to believe, it doesn't seem real; with a pain so deep, you can't describe how you feel. I have done it a few times; yet I know God is the reason I have this life of mine. God is the creator of me, you, and all of us, in him we must still put all of our trust. He has a reason for allowing things to be; even though we don't understand: God has all the power of life and death in his hand. There is nothing anyone can do; God will keep you strong, and he will pull you through; so don't stray away too long; return to God, and he will forgive all wrong. God can bring you joy, as well as allow you sorrow; he can instill in you hope, for a brand new tomorrow.

Brand New Day

I'm shouting "thank you lord" and saying it out loud; you let me wake to see another sun breaking through the clouds. I look out at the bright and beautiful sunshine, so radiant to see, it almost blinds. You have smiled upon the earth, and breathed new life into the children of your birth. You sent down your power from above, and touched me with your hand of love.

Let It Go

When I'm feeling anxious, I have to stop myself, because worry is no good for me or anyone else. I take a deep breath; calm my nerves, and let my frustration out; then give it to God, and after a while, there's no more to worry about. A feeling of sweet relief fills my body with confidence and peace.

Why I Do It

I don't write for money or fame; I do it to lift up Jesus' name. The money would be very nice; but I do it to try to change someone's life, by being a witness for Jesus Christ, because money can't give me eternal life. I know my days will come to a close; so I write the thoughts of my heart for both young and old. If I can help just one through my words; my mission is accomplished, because someone has heard.

THANKSGIVING PRAYER

Thank you Lord for my state of mind, for letting me be here one more time. Thank you for my family and friends, for the health and strength that they are in. Bless everyone all over this world; man, woman, boy and girl. Thank you for bringing me all the way, on yet another thanksgiving day.

KEEP YOUR FAITH

Out of all that you may go through; remember that God is there with you. Put your hand in his hand, ask him to help you to stand. Through all your sorrows and grief, only God can give you relief. Pray in your heart, or on your knees, ask God to have mercy in times like these.

Simply A Test

If you believe in my father, believe also in me; I am a part of the Trinity, father, son, and the holy ghost make three. When you begin to think that you don't need God; he will shake you up by making your life hard. God will let you know that without him, all you accomplish will come to woe. Everything that happens, God will allow, just to break you, and cause you to bow. He will bring you down, and put you through a test; just believe in him, and he will do the rest. If you believe that God is real, in due time all will be revealed.

After The Rain

After all the storm and rain; God blesses us with a new day to proclaim. The earth has been cleansed and everything is fresh and new; a bright and sunny day has been presented to you. All the magnificence and beauty is shown; through a new day created by God to his own. After the rain everything is fresh; the smell of the land, and the air of cleanliness. Earth's finest water that comes down as rain; God's gift to nature that springs forth life again. Appreciate the world before and after the rain,which God created for us since our time began.

BIRD WATCHING

I watched a bird just the other day, as he landed on the ground and headed my way; I didn't move or budge an inch; afraid he would fly away if caught in a pinch. I just watched him as he pecked around; hunting for food somewhere on the ground. I watched him, but he didn't watch me, he finally gave up and flew back up in a tree.

CHAPTER THREE

Let It Flow

Let the spirit of God freely flow; praise his name so that all will know; His love will cover you no matter where you go. He gives you the courage to be bold; when his peace is abiding in your soul. Let the spirit of God freely flow; he can lift you up when you are feeling low. Be a witness to his mighty power; that he sends down to us from his heavenly tower.

God Is

The one who gave up his life; to save us he paid the price. The one who was raised from the dead, and went back to his father as he had said. A healer in a time of pain; a shelter in the storm and rain. A comforter in a time of sorrow; the giver of all our tomorrows. The keeper of our soul; a mighty hand to hold. He's everywhere at the same time; the regulator of our mind. The one who wakes us everyday; the one all powerful in every way.

Life Travelers

As we travel down this road of life; we will have disappointments and strife. The curves and u- turns can cause us to lose sight of living for God and doing what is right.When we come into those u- turns and curves; just give it to God, and he will calm our nerves. With God's guidance we will not stray, because he is with us all the way. He will take the wheel on this road of life; if we trust in him, he will lead us to the light.

Pretender

You pretend to be all that, but God knows where your heart is at. You talk to hear yourself talk, but you do not walk the walk. If you truly mean well; others secrets you would not tell. You stand with others when it's convenient for you; half the things you claim, you do not do. You get mad when things don't go your way; then you sit quiet with nothing to say. You tell everything about someone else, but you never tell on yourself.

The New Normal

There is a virus that's plaguing the land; and each of us has to do what we can. This is our reality, to wear face masks and gloves to stay virus free. We can't bury our heads in the sand; we have to obey the laws of man, because God put the authority into their hands. To protect others, and ourselves too; we should do what we are required to do. Our freedom is limited from the things we normally do; this is a new normal that we have to get used to. Everything has changed from what it used to be; this is our reality; the way God has allowed it you see. This is the new normal of our days, until people repent of their wicked ways. This world will never be the same, until men accept the power and glory of Jesus' mighty name.

What Is Sown

What is sown, we will also reap, a promise from God that he will keep. If you intentionally do others wrong, you will certainly have to atone. You may not know how or when; but God is not pleased with any type of sin. You may think that you are getting away, but the time will come for you one day. God's word is true, and he cannot lie; he sees all that we do from his home on high.

Wait On Him

When you do all you can, and your situation just escalate; go to God in prayer, and patiently wait. He is listening, just don't give up; hold on to your faith, and in him trust; that's why your faith must remain strong; when it seems like it's just taking too long. I know that waiting can be very hard, but what else can you do, but wait on God. We don't have the power to control our own life; it is through God that we will win the fight. Just ask in prayer; trust, and wait; God is always there, he is the author of our fate.

In His Favor

Society today puts importance on who you are; the things you possess, and if you are a rising star. Unless your status has preceded you; they won't give you the credit due. By man's standards we are denied, and often looked over because of pride. God sees in us what others choose not to see; he knows our potential, and what all of us can be. We are highly favored in God's eyes, by living for him, we gain the eternal prize.

A Tiny Seed

God said if we have enough faith the size of a mustard seed; that is all the security we need. A mustard seed is a tiny thing, but from it many blessings will spring. A seed that's rooted will grow strong; with nourishment from God's word you won't go wrong. Our blessings will come down from God, because he knows what's in our hearts. Whatever life throws at us from day to day; we must trust God to make a way.

Perilous Times

When times get hard and full of unrest; it is God who will help us get through this test. Don't give in to Satan and lose your faith, but on God you have to wait. Satan cannot give you eternal life, or rescue you from your toil and strife; do not let him have power over you, by the help of Jesus you will make it through. Jesus died for you and me, so that from all our troubles we would be set free.

CHAPTER FOUR

Depressed

I keep telling myself when all hope seems lost, to hold my head up, because Jesus has already paid the cost. Whatever my situation, I am not alone; God is always with me, and he'll help me to hold on. I have to remember that everything will be alright; my hope is renewed; knowing God will handle my fight. The peace of mind and the safety I feel, is my assurance that my God is real.

When In Doubt

When we have doubt within our heart; it's hard for us to fully trust God. There were so many times I didn't understand; it was hard for me to realize that he was God and man. When I read his holy word; he opened up my understanding to all the teaching I had heard. We must believe within our heart, and trust that Jesus is the son of God. Sometimes we all have doubt, and think that God has left us out, but God has his own timeline, it's not the same as yours or mine.

I Wonder

Salvation is made possible by believing that Christ died and rose from the dead; this is what the bible said. I wonder if we consider all that God has done; when he gave up the life of his one and only son. I wonder if we meditate on the great love he has for us; when he created us out of the dust. I wonder if we truly believe; that God is the answer to all of our needs. I wonder when life is going good; we don't acknowledge God the way that we should. I wonder why we decide to pray; only when trouble is in our way. I wonder if your heart is true; when asking God to come help you. I wonder if your life will take on a different view, because of the storms God has brought you through. Sometimes I wonder if men can actually see; the power in his hands that caused all creation to be.

Memories Of You

As I take my final view; I will always have memories of you. There were good times as well as bad; without you being in my life, there would be no memories to be had. You were a blessing in so many ways, and I will cherish those memories the rest of my days.

Grief

When you lose a child; the hurt is deep and strong; you are surrounded by people, yet you feel empty and alone; you don't look forward to the next day, your reason for living has been taken away. We go through the motions of our daily life; but nothing has meaning, and nothing seems right. God gives, and God takes away; he didn't put them in your life to stay. He knows your mind and how you feel; it was done according to his will. God heals all wounds through time and prayer; he fills the emptiness, and let's you know he's always there.

Another You

It just hurts me deep inside; when people I've known all my life get puffed up with pride. I asked myself the reason why; when they started to change as time went by. They cling to greener pastures once they get their feet in the door; and will not associate in their friend zone anymore. They forget everything they've ever been taught; seeking acceptance that can't be bought. Too much pride will eventually bring them down; the ones they were trying to impress, won't even come around. How is it they don't understand; to be true to oneself, is to look to God and not man.

My Minds Eye

As I look out my window at the pouring rain; I think of so much sadness and pain. The raindrops to me seem like countless tears, of all those that mourn throughout the years. So many tears that can never be numbered; the strong, as well as the weak have been made to humble. God will bring you through all the pain when it gets too hard; time heals all wounds by the help of God.

Meditation

As I sit alone on this awesome day; looking through my window as I ponder my way. All is quiet, the sun is shining bright; it is a crisp Monday morning that makes everything seem so right. When the dark clouds loom within; I ask myself, will it ever end. I get so wrapped up in the world of material things, and lose sight of all the trouble they bring. When my trials get heavy, and weigh me down; I look up to Heaven to the only one that can lift me up from the ground.

Nature's Wonder

As the wind blows wildly through the trees; limbs sway rapidly in the breeze. The song they sing is of rustling leaves. The beauty of nature is all around; it grabs my attention with a subtle sound. The wonder of creation is everywhere you look; from the smallest insect to a stream with a babbling brook. Take time to be thankful, and appreciate the wonders God has made; because this fleeting life will very soon fade.

This Too Shall Pass

God will bring you through your storms, and give you the strength to bear; he is a God of mercy, he will always be there. It may seem like he doesn't hear; but he is listening when your prayers are sincere. You just have to trust and wait, no matter how long it may take. He is a God that comes in the nick of time; he is the one true vine. He will clear your storms away, and raise you up to a brighter day.

CHAPTER FIVE

God Forgives

Lord help us to grasp the greatness, and majesty of your power; you are with us every minute and every hour. We are so unfaithful, and continually transgress; yet you still put up with us and all our mess. You don't have to travel from place to place, to forgive the sins of this human race; your power is so vast, and so wide, all over this world you reside. If we would just meditate on the glory you possess; we would be able to stand up to life's tests. You are all powerful; all knowing; all seeing; you are the life force of all human beings.

He Gives Gifts

Everyone has a talent, even if we don't realize it yet; through God our talents are already present. We have to grow into the realization; the talent that comes natural to us without hesitation. A gift that God gives, no one can steal. It is not hard if it comes from God. We must make an effort to embrace our gift, which was given to us, and designed to uplift. Don't be afraid to let God take the lead; a spiritual gift will always succeed. A special talent is given to everyone; ask God for enlightenment, and it shall be done.

October Rain

The sun and blue skies have been hidden away; the rain it seems to have come to stay. Cloudy skies and rainy days, have lasted two weeks to my amazement. October rain is pouring so much, it chills the body just from the touch. Sitting inside and looking out, at overcast skies round about; the day seems lonely in a way; with colors of pale and misty gray. October rain has lasted so long, it won't be missed when it is gone.

It's A Boy

Do you know the baby boy; born into the world to bring salvation and joy. His father sent him from above, because he created us out of love. He wanted to give us another chance, so his son came down in the form of a man. He started when he was very young; preaching salvation to everyone. He wanted to bring us out of the dark, by putting his light into our heart. He left his home to pay for our sins, so that we could have life again. He became the sacrifice, and his name is Jesus Christ.

Approaching Night

The beautiful skyline of orange and blue hues, stretched across the edge of a clear blue sky; the setting of the sun indicating that another day has gone by. The sun must give way to the darkness of night, and descend into the heavens with its bright glowing light. It's had it's time to shine upon the earth, and must close out the day for nightfalls rebirth.

I'm Rich

I am rich in the blessings God gives; each day I awake because he lives. I am rich because of the peace he brings, by not letting me stress over material things. I am rich because he hears my prayer; he is never missing in action, he is always there. I am rich under his protection; I am rich because he guides my direction. I am rich because I have a portion of my health and strength; I am rich because all my blessings are heaven sent. I am rich in knowing that I serve a God; through whom all things are possible, and nothing is too hard.

Sunshine

Thank you for all the blessings you send my way, as I awake to the bright sunshine of a brand new day to feel the warmth of its glorious ray. It shines so bright up in the sky; you can't look at it with the naked eye. The sun is essential for our well being, and all forms of life that spring from its healing. Without the sun there would be no light, and we would be living in a continuous night.

The Coming Storm

I have often looked up at the sky, and saw a flock of birds quickly flying by. I can hear their chirping, as they gracefully fly; sailing across an ominous sky. Even the birds can sense a coming storm; they call out to the others, so they can be warned. I see no birds when the storm is raging, but when it's safe, they leave their safe haven. The skies are clear, the storm has passed; the birds are flying again at last.

Low Esteem

I didn't have fine clothes when I was in school; I looked at others as being the exception to the rule. My self esteem was very low; I got to a point where I didn't even want to go. I didn't talk about it with anyone else, and didn't want them to know how I really felt. I didn't think I was as good as the others because of who I was; short in stature, and being teased for that cause. I was so self conscious, I hated being me, until God opened my eyes one day, and allowed me to see; he created us all out of love whether we are short or tall. I am just as important, no matter what my height. My self esteem became strong because of God's wonderful light.

Open Your Mind

How great thou art oh Lord; you spoke to my mind, and I heard your voice. You sounded like a natural man, and spoke in words I could understand. My eyes opened wide from the words you said, as you awakened me from my bed. Never stop listening, and you will find; God speaks to the heart as well as the mind; sometimes in the midnight hour; at other times according to his divine power.

Never Say Never

There are things we say we would never do, but how can we know that this is true? Suppose a situation arise that take you completely by surprise. We do exactly what we said we wouldn't; with no thought of whether we should or shouldn't. Something we never would expect, could happen to us as well as the next.

CHAPTER SIX

My Sustainer

Lord, when I think of how you have blessed me down through the years; my eyes are filled with joyful tears. You have provided me with my strength and health; took care of my needs like no one else. I have seen others go through so much suffering and pain; you brought them out to give witness to your name. I can not say that I know what they went through, but I give praise because I know what you can do. Lord, I pray that whatever I must go through; keep me strong in my faith in you. I must depend on you in my darkest hour of day or night; you are my salvation, and the keeper of my life.

When Mother Is There

When mother is there, she will always care. When mother is there she will keep you in her prayers. When mother is there she'll lend a helping hand, and encourage you to do the best in life you can. She will support you through thick and thin, no matter how much trouble you get in. Mother is there when you are all alone, out of money, and your friends are gone. Mother is there whenever you call, to pick you up when you take a fall. When mother is there you always know; there is a place that you can go. It's truly a blessing to have a mother there; who will help you no matter what, when, or where.

The Old House

The house I once occupied stands empty and alone, as if it had died since I've been gone. All around the area it seems so gray; some of the people that were there when I left have even moved away. The house that holds so many memories from back then; now stands lonely, without a friend. The windows are like eyes that look out at me, as if to ask the question, how can this be? Even with all its holes and cracks; I miss the old house, but I don't want to go back.

What's On Your Mind

God knows us better than we know ourselves, he knows our ways and actions better than anyone else. He knows the desires of our hearts; the next thing we'll do before we even start. He knows every hair on our head; every thought in our mind before it's even said. If our thoughts are evil or good; nothing is hidden from God, although we wish it would. No man knows what's on another man's mind, but God knows what we are thinking at all times.

Open Your Ears

Whomever has ears let them hear; the word of God that's very clear. You cannot serve two masters, for one leads to eternal life, and the other to disaster. Consider the path in life you take; one is love, and the other hate. Whatever it is that we may do, God will be there because his love is true. He knows our sinful nature you see; still he chose to set us free; give praise to God for all to see, no straddling the fence for you or me. Open your ears that you may hear; if you are living for God, you have nothing to fear.

No Time To Waste

There is an urgency to do all we can while we are here on this earthly land. We cannot lay up in our bed unless we are sick; time is constantly passing, and the days go by quick. We must go about our day and let God guide the way. We must be concerned about others, and not just ourselves, because what God has for us, it will always be left. We must encourage those that are weak, and let God guide us in what we speak; give support to those who cannot stand; we are all weak as a natural man. We must lift up Jesus whenever we can; tell the unbeliever of his divine plan. There are some that may not even know; how to seek salvation, or what it takes to grow. Don't waste time holding a grudge; forgive one another, and offer each other a hug. We have no time to waste on this earthly plain; we must lift up Jesus, and proclaim his name.

Constant Prayer

Sometimes a prayer consumes my thoughts, and everything around me seems to get lost. People and things just disappear, when prayers go up for God to hear. A constant prayer always in mind, is thank you Lord for this lifetime. Constantly thanking him throughout the day; for walking with me along the way. Thanking him for keeping me strong; when nothing goes right and all goes wrong. I thank him for helping me to cope; when it feels like I'm at the end of my rope. I thank him for keeping me safe; always remembering that it's only by his grace.

Winds

Gusty winds so wild and free; can't be contained by you or me. Wind that is harsh against the skin; can cause the human body to bend. Wind so strong it sweeps the street; can pick the body up off its feet. Wind with no form or shape; can uproot a tree or demolish a state. Wind that blows everywhere, wild and free without a care. Wind you can't see with the natural eye, only by what it touches as it blows them by.

Own Your Salvation

Pay no attention to the person behind the mask, whose attitude changes and does not last. Only on Sunday do they give God the praise, but what about the other six days. They forget about God and won't even mention his name, when around certain people; they act as if they are ashamed. The light of a Christian will always shine through, in all your conversations, and by the things you do. Never let anyone steal your joy; it's just one of Satan's ploys. Own your salvation no matter where you are; never be ashamed to let others know that God is your super star.

The Human Condition

Nobody could redeem us but the son, without him, it would have never been done. We would still be lost in our sin, with no hope of redemption out of the trouble we were in. God's love gave us a chance to call upon him and change our circumstances. He sent his son to take it all on, to suffer and die for all of our wrong. The human condition is to wallow in sin; instead of repentance for salvation to begin. We have to pray for forgiveness, and seek out Christ, if we hope to gain eternal life.

CHAPTER SEVEN

Children Of The King

We are children of the king; the creator of all things that be, the author of our destiny. We are children of the king; the holy one of whom we sing. We are children of the king; the one on whom we can always lean. We are children of the king; who gives us protection under his wing. The one who said "let us make man", the one who holds the whole world in his hand. The one who provides for us day and night, and guides us through this path of life. We are children of the king; the one by whom all things are done; the one true God, the only one.

The Tie That Binds.

When mother and child have formed a bond; the welfare of her child is her only concern. A true mother doesn't think of herself, but puts her child before anything else. From birth through the childhood years, mother is there to soothe the bruise and kiss away the tears. When you become a woman or man, mother is still doing all she can. Mother is there through good times and bad; when your friends aren't around that you thought you had. Keep in mind this is a true mother; caring and loving, unlike any other. Mother and child have an unbreakable bond; in life or death, the bond lives on.

Shattered Dreams

Shattered dreams are like broken glass, to put together is a difficult task. Like a puzzle when a piece is gone; something is missing; something is wrong. Well laid plans of women and men, can't be put together again. Shattered dreams like an ocean wave; gone with the tide, and can't be saved.

Be Yourself

At all times be yourself; never try to be like anyone else. Whatever another person may do; may not be the thing that's suited for you. No two people are alike, you see, that's the difference between you and me.

The Tree

There's something about a Christmas tree; that warms the heart for all to see. A special warmth it seems to give, with all the lights and fancy frills. It brightens the face of adults and children, and fills with joy their every smile.

Images

Once you have studied an object's face; the image of them is hard to erase. Close your eyes and you will find; the image of them still in your mind. Images of people you've always known, those related that are dead and gone. Images of things you've wanted to buy; you never got them, and wonder why. Images of animals you have seen; you go to bed, and they are in your dreams. Images will always last; you deal with them as time goes past.

Housewarming

Accept this gift from me to you, it is something I wanted to do. I have wanted to do this for so long; ever since you moved into your new home. I had to wait and bide my time, this is for both of you who have been so kind. Knowing you both has been a pleasure; a feeling that I cannot measure. You have always treated me like one of your own, and always had time to talk when I called on the telephone. My children love to be around you, I must tell you that I do too. God has brought us from a mighty long way; I thank him for knowing you each and every day.

Someone

Someone has told me of the world and the earth; someone has told me the day of my birth. Someone has told me of the mom and the dad; someone has told me of the good and the bad. Someone has told me the difference between the truth and a lie; someone has told me of a tiny baby's cry. Someone has told me of animals and trees; someone has told me of the birds and the bees. Someone has told me we will reap what we sow; someone has told me in nature all things grow. Someone has told me the twelve months of the year; someone has told me of holiday cheer. Someone has told me of death and the grave; someone has told me how a soul can be saved. Someone has told me of hate and love; someone has told me of God up above. Someone has told me of Jesus Christ; someone has told me how he gave up his life. Someone has told me how Christ rose from the dead; someone has told me about the life on earth he led. Someone has told me of all these things; someone on whom I could always lean. (my mother).

Child Abuse

Child abuse is an unspeakable thing, because of all the suffering it brings. Children subjected to child abuse, feel that they are of no more use; afraid to love, and afraid to trust; surviving only because they must. Children who don't know where to turn; because of this they decide to run. Children abused until they are grown, can become abusers of their own.

Tears

How many tears are there in all, of both you too who are very small; you who cry every morning in the week. How many tears must I seek.

Long Ago

I've never forgotten when I was small; I was your girl out of them all. I remember times that I spent the night; of being afraid when you cut off the light. I remember being awakened at the break of day, to the sound of a rooster, and the mules bay. I remember eggs cooked sunny side up; that I tried to eat, but didn't like very much. I remember sitting on the front porch swing; in a white nylon dress that I wore that spring. Memories like these can not be measured; they are mine of you to be always treasured.

Condolences

There are no words that can ease your pain; but I pray for your strength in Jesus name. I know it's hard and the pain is great; just lean on the lord to be strong in faith. I hurt with you in your time of grief, but as time goes past God will give you relief.

Welcome

Welcome to one and all; to the house of the Lord, where no one is small. God told us to love one another, because everyone here is the next man's sister or brother. Feel free to sing, talk, shout,or pray; just praise the lord in your own special way. Rain, sleet, snow, or sunshine; you are welcome here at any time.

Never Give Up

Never give up when life gets hard; nothing is impossible through the will of God. On him you can depend and lean; he will be there to intervene. He has brought you from the past until now; he has always made a way for you somehow. Think back on what he did for you then, he is the same as he has always been. Patiently wait, and in his own time, he will put your troubles behind. I know sometimes it all seems hopeless, but God is on your side; so never give up, just keep your hope alive.

Time For Celebration

Come! Let us celebrate our Savior's birth, for all that he's done while here on earth. Even though he was mocked and scorned; he had a job to do, and many miracles he did perform. He went back to heaven to prepare us a place, when we get to heaven to see God's blessed face. Let us celebrate like the angels did above; singing glory to God in the highest, because of his wondrous love.

With God

With God impossible does not exist; there is no situation too hard for him to fix. With God you can have peace of mind, even in the hardest of times. With God there is love and forgiveness for all; not a select few, according to your judgement call. With God you won't always be stressed out; that's what his perfect peace is all about. With God you won't worry about things you can't change; calm down, turn it over to him, and don't complain. With God, if you let him take control; you will see his work begin to unfold.

CHAPTER EIGHT

Another Chance

To save mankind he was born into the world; his mother was Mary, a virgin girl. God is the father, as well as the son; through his power conception was done. He preached a new covenant for man to hear, a plan of salvation to draw us near. If we would believe in Jesus the son; that he died for everyone. He wants us all to believe and trust, through love for his creation, he did this for us.

Say Amen

If you are a member of the christian band; open your mouth and say amen; when you know the truth is being told, it's just a blessing to your soul. Say amen, or simply wave your hand; praise the lord while you still can. Give witness to the truth and say amen, but for God just take a stand, we are all included in his divine plan. Let the spirit guide you in all your ways; lift up your voice in joyful praise.

TRACKS OF LIFE

The tracks of our steps will be washed away, with the rain from heaven that falls each day, we are not put on this earth to stay. The impact we have on others lives, will live in their memory and always abide. The loved ones that we leave behind, will always carry us in their minds. Our tracks on land will disappear, but the footprints on the heart will always be here.

Who Are You Following

If you are not applying God's will to your life; how can you say you are following Christ? Why waste your time coming to hear the word; if you are not studying and living according to what you have heard. We must have love and compassion for everyone. God loves us all, and requires us to do the same. If we are following Christ, there can be no favoritism; we must apply all of his ways into our daily living.

Consider This

Consider all that you are able to do; it's just not possible without God allowing you. Nothing can be accomplished without God in your life, you have no control; so let him lead you into the light. You can't fix things all on your own; only God has the power to right any wrong. We need God each and every day, he can speak a word and all will be washed away.

Torn

I am trying to support others, but I feel guilty in doing so; I know what the law says, and yet I still go. I can do nothing but turn to God; go on with my life, and keep him in my heart. He knows how I feel, and if my commitment to him is real. I don't have to prove myself to anyone but God, by living a daily life with love and compassion in my heart. God's word tells us to obey the laws of the land; one way or another we all must take a stand. When every knee takes a bow; God will heal the land; he will remove the touch of evil with his mighty hand.

When We Pray

We may not have been able to get to the building, but the church should be in our heart; all the while we were absent, we should have been thanking and praising God. Through all the death and sickness going on; God is the one who keeps us strong. I pray for all people; strong and weak, that God's mercy is what we should seek. If we would remember what God said; we wouldn't be filled with so much dread. He is the only one that can stop the pain of death and plague that pours down like rain. No matter how bad things get; God will never leave us, so there's no need to fret.

A Light In The Darkness

God is a mystery in which we will never understand; all we can do is believe and trust in his divine plan. We are to be his light in a world dark with sin; we must reflect that light in order to draw sinners in. A light that will guide them along the right path, to God who forgives all sins and puts away their past. Let us be a light so those lost can find their way, from a dark and lonely place that the world is offering today.

God Controls All

When we lose a friend or loved one to sickness, accident, or any other violent way; we choose to blame God, and turn ourselves away. We ask God why? Why did you let my friend or relative die?. It's so hard to believe, it doesn't seem real; with a pain so deep, you can't describe how you feel. God is the creator of you, me, and all of us, in him we must still put our trust. He has his reasons for allowing things to be, even though we don't understand; God has all the power of life and death in his hand. There is nothing anyone can do; God will keep you strong, and he will pull you through. Don't stay away too long; return to God, he will forgive all wrong. God can give you joy as well as allow you sorrow; he can instill in you hope for a brand new tomorrow.

No Such Luck

It's not by our power that we do anything, but by the power of God and the mercy he brings. We often say" I got lucky or it was just my luck" We don't recognize that it was God's touch. There is no such thing as good or bad luck; God is always in the plan, we can do nothing by our own hands.

Jesus Is Waiting

If you are living a sinful life and have not accepted Jesus Christ; he is always near if you are ready and sincere. He wants you to come, no matter what you have done. No one else can forgive our sins, or renew our hearts to start again. When the troubles of life begin to take its toll; he is the only one that can bring peace to your soul. The time is now to make your plea; tomorrow is not a guarantee. He is the one on whom to depend; the only one since time began.

Set Apart

As Christians we are set apart, and called upon to live for God; to follow the example of Jesus Christ, as we live out our daily life. Set apart to love everyone no matter who it is, or what they have done. Set apart to keep down confusion of any kind; come together in agreement, and be of one mind. Set apart because we are free, from the sting of death that hung over you and me. Set apart to walk this narrow way; with Satan constantly trying to lead us astray. We are set apart, because God has poured out his spirit into our heart.

CHAPTER NINE

Lifeforce

Sometimes I realize, I didn't thank God the minute I opened my eyes. Even before my feet hit the floor, I should have thanked God for watching over me once more. He is the life force that keeps me strong; he gives me movement throughout muscle and bone. Sometimes I get caught up in personal stuff, and I just don't thank him enough. I get so comfortable in my own life; I forget his life force is what keeps me day and night. Thank you for all things, big and small, for hearing my prayer whenever I call. His life force is the reason I am alive; without it I could not survive. I thank him for family and everyone, and ask for his guidance till each day is done.

Assurance

I am at peace and without fear; knowing that God is always near. I know in my heart that his word is true; that is my assurance that he'll do what he said he would do. He will guide and let me know, the right way that I should go. He keeps me strong throughout the day, as I go along my way. Even within the long hours of night, I am never out of his sight. I feel his presence all around; a blessed assurance of a mind that's sound.

Always Aware

We've all got to leave this earth, no doubt about that, and I want to be where Jesus is at. If I do what he commands of me, it is his face in heaven I want to see. If I live this life on earth by telling others of Jesus' birth. If I am able to guide them to Christ, by telling them of his death and life. To be rooted and focused on him; to let others know that God forgives, and does not condemn. To let others know that he washes all sins away; just trust in him, and get out of their own way.

No Assumptions

I take nothing for granted because without God; life wouldn't be possible without the love in his heart. I thank God for every day I wake; for letting me love instead of hate. I thank him for all the blessing he sends my way, for just letting me be able to say; thank you Lord for this new day. I take nothing for granted because I know; this life is limited, and filled with woe. My God is with me, and he sees and knows all; he will pick me up when I take a big fall. He is the one who continually provides, he will never leave my side. I take nothing for granted because I can do nothing myself; I am here by God's grace and mercy, no one else.

Through New Eyes

Appreciate the world while you can, that God created for the habitation of man. The beauty of creation displayed everyday, all arranged in a beautiful array. Plants, animals, flowers, and trees; all put here to serve our needs. Some of us have eyes to see and yet; we pay no attention to when the sun rise or set. This world is only a loan; appreciate its beauty before you are gone. Look at the world through new eyes, and realize the awesomeness that God supplies. Appreciate the world while you can; see through new eyes the beauty of this land.

The Church Is Not A Playground

The building is a place of worship, where we come to hear the word; every child of God should have respect, so it can be heard. Be considerate of those around you; don't distract them from hearing God's truth. Pay attention to what's being said; God's word is trying to be fed. Grownups seem to just be waiting to get to church to start their conversation. Cell phones should be turned off; tablets left at home; stop sitting up in church talking, and playing on the phone. Once we come inside those doors; our focus should be on God and nothing more. Leave all the worldly things outside; give all your praise to the one who died.

Everlasting Love

If we would truly open our heart; to fully trust in the love of God, we could feel his presence everyday, walking with us along the way. Even when we lie down at night; we know he's watching over us, and everything will be alright. We have the assurance God is with us at all times; he takes away whatever it is clouding our minds. Maybe then we could comprehend an eternal love that has no end.

A WORLD OF TROUBLE

There's enough trouble in the world today; without Christians fighting each other to get their own way. God is allowing Satan to put you through a test, and he will do his very best. He will cause disruptions in every area of your life, to get you to give up and turn away from Christ. We must be strong, and not conform to this world; keep your faith and hope alive, because this world is in so much peril.

Why Am I Here

Why am I here? Why was I born; to tell who will listen, this is why we were formed. God gave us life out of his love; he gave us freewill to choose him above. We have a commission in this life; to serve and worship him in the world's sight. To let others see Christ working through us; to build up their hope, so that in God they will trust. If you do not have that zeal; you mission will not have any yield. Be real in your mission, whatever it is, and your rewards will be heaven filled.

What's On The Inside

We dress the outside of our bodies to make ourselves look good; then act prim and proper the way we think we should. We decorate the outside, but the inner self is what we hide. Men and women alike; your makeup, or jewelry overshadow who you really are, because it shines so bright. What's on the inside will eventually come out, and those you have often fooled will now know what you are about. They will slowly gravitate away from you, because you are not who they thought they knew.

Spiritual Realm

The spirit and very essence of me, will one day be in a place of peace and tranquillity. None but the righteous will enter in; A place where there will be no more sin. There will be nothing to fear; no more crying or shedding a tear. No more poor or bad health; no more sickness, and no more death. There will be no locked doors; I can walk around free on heaven's floors. No more worries of any kind; a state of being, and peace of mind. Giving praise day and night, to a God of grace, mercy, and life.

CHAPTER TEN

I Need Thee

When I'm in my spiritual place; I think of heaven and God's amazing grace. I think about how good God is to me and tears fill my eyes, because without him, I would not be able to survive. Whatever trials come upon me in life; I Look to him to help me fight. I can't fight the battles on my own, but God has the power to do it alone, and he helps me to just hold on. I just can't do anything by myself, it's all in God's hands, and no one else.

Pray Without Ceasing

Do not let the day go by without giving God thanks, because he is the reason why we are able to get out of bed, and have the activity of our arms and legs. He gives us the strength to do all things; he is worthy, our king of kings. If you haven't thanked God today; take a moment just to pray. Speak the words within your mind, it doesn't have to be verbal all the time. We all just need to stop and say; thank you Lord for another beautiful day.

Truth Be Told

When someone tells you what the bible says; they are interpreting it in their own way; they may be right, or they may be wrong, that's why we must read it on our own. Ask God to reveal the mystery of his word to you, so you will know if what they are telling you is true. If you just hear and never seek; how can you grow strong instead of weak? You will follow every doctrine you hear; be led astray because it sounded sincere. Don't just believe everything you are told; find out for yourself to protect your soul.

Everyday

Everyday is a day that God has given us, to be thankful for all that he does, and in him put our trust. Everyday is a day of praise, to give God thanks for all of our days. Everyday is a chance to start anew; to treat others right the way God wants us to. Everyday is a chance to tell someone about Christ; how he died, so that we would have life. Everyday is a chance to be a blessing to someone else, if we would just stop focusing on ourself. Everyday is a day to search our own heart, to make sure that our lives are within the will of God. Everyday God lets us see, is a chance to be the best that we can be.

Motions Of Life

We are going through the motions of life, but we are not living if we don't know Jesus Christ. Each day we go through the same routine, but have we thought about letting others know how they can be redeemed. Living life on our own basis, is a day gone by that we have wasted. God gives us this time to use our mouth; to let the unsaved know what living life is about. Life is more than the motions itself; it is to be lived in a way that will help guide someone else.

Why Worry

Why worry about something that hasn't happened yet? You are doing nothing but getting yourself upset. Worrying beforehand is certainly not good, and worry itself can drain your livelihood; you just can't think straight the way that you should. You can't add one day to your life; worrying about things that don't go right. All that worry will have been in vain; what exactly would you have gained?

Nine One One

Let us remember nine one one, and all the damage that was done. The devastation and agony it cost, on that day so many lives were lost. Family and friends were torn apart; through the senseless act of man's evil heart. A day that will live on in our minds, as we remember those left behind. With heavy hearts, we reflect upon that day; always remembering that God is just a prayer away.

Exercise Your Right

There was a time when we didn't have a voice; as black people, we weren't allowed to have that choice. Our ancestors fought for those rights, so we would be recognized in this life. It makes me sad to hear black people say, "Honey I don't vote, they're going to get who they want anyway." We have every opportunity to cast our vote; early voting, polls, and absentee; our ancestors were slaves, but we are free; exercise your right to be. If we don't fight for change, everything will remain the same. Our strengths is our voice; we can make a difference, and we have that choice. No matter who they choose; one vote determines whether a person win or lose.

What We Possess

Possessions don't have a mind of their own; they are not made of flesh and bone. We love them, but they can't love us, they are a side effect of our lust. Possessions will be here when you and I are gone; the things we hold on to for so long. We will surely leave them behind, to be thrown, sold, or given away with time. Possessions shouldn't be your life long goal, but to gain salvation through the regeneration of your soul.

Auld Lang Syne

There is sadness and joy in auld lang syne; which ends the old and rings in a new time. Should old acquaintances be forgotten, and never brought to mind, or do we recall both sad and happy times. People we have known for many years; some have passed on, and some still live. Each and every person has had an impact on our life in some way; we are all passing through, we were not put here to stay. Old acquaintances should never be forgotten, and often brought to mind; the years may pass, but true friends and loved ones will be remembered throughout our lifetime. Make new friends, but remember the old; those are memories more precious than gold.

Choose Wisdom

The book of Proverbs is a teaching tool; full of life lessons you won't learn in school. It's an instruction for both young and old, on how to live your life by seeking wisdom for your soul. Pray for understanding and knowledge that you may stay strong; try to help those whom you know are doing wrong. Listen to what the Lord has to say; do not live your life following the wrong way; fear the Lord and choose to obey. Wisdom is what we all should seek, for wisdom will guide us to a life of goodwill and peace.

Autumn Leaves

Looking up and staring out, at nature's beauty all about; the power of God is all I see; showing through all that surrounds me. The splendor and height of the trees that reach high; as if to say" we are climbing to the sky". I imagine their roots run deep into the ground; strong and sturdy, hard to be found. Sing me a song oh graceful trees; a melody of your changing leaves. Sing out your colors of red, brown, yellow and gold; what a beautiful sight of nature to behold.

Victory

We have the victory, because Jesus died to set us free; the victory to overcome, through faith in God and his only son. He freed our soul, and gave us a choice; to follow him and be guided by his voice. The victory is an assurance that he is always there, to listen and hear our every prayer. The victory of not being afraid when we lie down to sleep; knowing that our soul is his to keep. The victory of not letting trouble get us down, by focusing on him to keep our mind sound. A victory won when he gave up his life, for all humanity, because no one else could pay the price.

Live, Love, Laugh

Live to laugh, and love to live; there is so much you have to give. Live to love, and love to laugh; forget about things that happened in the past. Embrace this life as much as you can; toward helping out your fellow man. Don't be hindered by a few aches and pains; remember that God forever reigns. Laugh a little every day, and God will chase those pains away. Live your life to the fullest, as a testimony to God and his great goodness.

Slumber Or Sleep

Our God never sleeps; he hears our prayers and sees us when we weep. He knows what we need even before we ask; he knows all about our present and our past. Be honest when you pray; he will know if you are truthful in the things you say. Just look up to heaven where your help comes from; when life seems to be coming undone. He will answer your prayer if your heart is true; turn to him, he will see you through. When things get so heavy, you can't seem to bear; just remember, he is right there.

Empty

I never put down on paper what my heart could feel; at the time God called you home, it seemed so unreal. I was on the outside looking in, at a world moving on I couldn't comprehend. Surrounded by people, yet I felt so alone; like no one else existed since you were gone. The house that was once your home took my breath away when I entered it alone. I saw no reason to get out of bed, to repeat another day filled with dread. I saw you in every young man that went by; I have no reason as to why. There was a hole I could not fill; I was so empty, and had no will; by the grace of God I began to heal. He slowly brought me back to myself; by his power only, and no one else. You will live on in my heart and mind, and won't be erased even with time.

IN MEMORIAM

CYRIL GRAY CARTER

CHAPTER ELEVEN

My Mindset

When my mind is on God; I begin to write because the words fill my heart. My mind is calm as I consider his power; I just write in that very hour. All things made, and all things that will come to be, is by his mighty power that shows all around me. I think of this beautiful world, and all therein; what he did to pay for mankind's sins. I think of his glory, and I just write, because he has been good to me all my life. I just write, because I know; one day my words will help someone else to grow.

My Legacy

God gave me a new direction; to write poetry that has a spiritual connection. A God given gift that comes from within; that keeps me at peace in my own skin. The very thoughts of my inner mind overwhelm me from time to time. Without my poetry; I am not myself, I can only be me, and no one else. I thank God for inspiring me, for bringing out in me what I could not see. When I am in that spiritual zone; my poems are a release from all that is wrong. I give praise to God's awesome power; everything in nature, down to the tiniest flower. This is my legacy, the poems I write for all to see; just know that hope should always be kept alive; God will accept you into his kingdom and give you an eternal prize. My legacy may not mean much to you, but this is my passion, and what God has called me to do. This is what I leave behind; to let you know that God is all things, to all people, at all times.

(Song) All Inclusive

If you love the Lord! Don't you know that your burdens will get lighter and lighter and lighter (chorus) loving, believing,and trusting, and waiting on him. If you believe in him, he'll make a way for you; out of no way. (repeat chorus) If you trust in him; you know that all things are possible only through him.(repeat chorus) If you wait upon him; you know that he will come on time, just when you need him.(repeat chorus.)

Old Things

If God has created in you a new heart, and you are a true believer in God; your old ways are left behind; never to constantly occupy your mind. The things of this world should not be what you crave, but the desire to live right, because through Christ you are saved. The things that you need; God will freely give, if we would just look up to him and live. Your old character should no longer be; but a new creature for all to see.

Nature's Embrace

Spring, summer, fall, and winter; nature's embrace is front and center. She wraps me in her sunshine when the earth is cold. She rains down her beautiful leaves in the fall of the year that comes from the trees. When the ground is hot and dry; a refreshing rain is welcomed from the sky. She gives us flowers in a beautiful array; birds that are chirping and singing away. Ice cycles reflecting in the sun; shining like crystals before the day is done. Nature's embrace is all around us, in a variety of emotions that are felt and touched.

Contemplation

Lord! As I look around this day; watching children laugh and play; people walking and talking and going about their way. All I can think about is your mercy and grace, that allows us to still be in this race. Sometimes I get weak in the faith because of my human frailties, and I have to just pray. If only we could comprehend the powerful love you have for all men. I pray for mankind to have a discerning mind, to know that your grace is sufficient; that all their blessings are heaven sent. I look up toward heaven and contemplate on your awesome power, and think of all the blessings on us that you shower.

Broken Trust

A person's word is said to be their bond; giving your word is just a gesture to some; they have no intentions of doing what needs to be done. If you don't do your very best, to stand on your word you will lose others' respect. Your word should not be given lightly, but with a sincere heart to help someone rightly. Your word is a reflection of the person you are; to break that trust will leave a scar. A broken trust is hard to rely on; their confidence in you is already gone.

We Can Do Nothing

Until all men recognize the power of God; nothing they do is going to work, we are all in for a world of hurt. Some take all the credit for what they do, without giving God the praise for allowing them to. God gave men the knowledge to do many things, but men can't stop the sickness, and death that this virus brings. These vaccines won't work unless it's God's will; only he can stop this virus, and make it be still. We certainly cannot help ourself, we must turn to God, and no one else. When men start to think they don't need God; he will show them his power through trials that are hard. We can do nothing without the power of God; pray for him to heal this land, by stretching out his mighty hand.

Flight Of The Dove

When Noah sent a dove to find dry land; all of this was in God's plan. Water was still covering the ground; on the dove's first flight; dry land could not be found. On the dove's second flight, water still covered the ground; with nowhere to land, the dove turned around. Seven days later, the dove flew again; returned with an olive branch as a sign there would soon be dry land. One week later the dove flew again; still searching for dry land; this time it did not return; the water receded, and dry land had begun. Twelve and a half months went by, before the earth was completely dry. Noah took his family and animals of every kind; left the ark to begin again; the earth was ready to be inhabited by man.

THE EGO OF MAN

There was nothing before God; the earth and sky did not make itself; God the father did it with his son's help. Man cannot contemplate, and all powerful God with a heart full of love instead of hate. Just because they cannot see; they refuse to accept how this can be. Man would like to think that he is in control; that he is the captain of his own soul. Man cannot command the sun to shine, or the moon to glow; he cannot cause plants and flowers to grow. Man could not place the moon, stars, and sun; they were spoken into existence, and it was already done. Man is just a helpless tool; without the power of God's command and rule.

A Change In Me

Once upon a bright sunny day like this; I awoke to an earth I didn't know exist. My hands and feet, they all looked new. Everything around me I saw in a new light; trees, grass, fresh and bright. A calming peace filled me inside, and the anxiousness I could not hide. I felt so special because God so loved me he forgave my sins, and gave me a chance for a new life to begin.

The Only Hope

This world is turned upside down, when those in government can't even find common ground. Everything that's gone wrong in this land, is all through the evilness of man. Satan has caused us to become cold and hard; by turning our hearts away from God. Don't put all your hope in man; they will disappoint you; God is limitless, there's nothing he can't do. Of this one thing I am sure; that God is our only cure.

Of One Mind

Two minds can't continue in the same body. When there is a constant tug of war; the body will break down and be no more. As one body we must all think alike; one can't go left, and the other go right. We must act responsibly; come together and all agree. If our minds are on a different plain; there is no unity in praising Jesus' name. The body of Christ must be of one mind, in order to have an impact on mankind.

CHAPTER TWELVE

Snowdance

The sun is heating up the snow, slowly melting it as the day goes. A trickle to the left, and a trickle to the right; turning it to water before my sight. A slow motion here, and a fox trot there; twisting and turning and running everywhere. It dribbles off the rooftop in a tiny little stream; then it drops to the ground so clear and clean. Snow radiates the earth as it glistens in the sun; once it's gone, the dance is done.

Daughterisms

She is very independent, and does not rely on a man to validate her; being responsible for herself is what she would prefer. She looks to God to guide her through, in everything she attempts to do. She is loyal to her friends if they treat her right, and a good friend to have in your life. She is very determined, and very smart; things that are easy for her, to me seem hard. She is very sensitive as well, and others secrets she will not tell. She is very affectionate to the ones she loves; is always giving them kisses and hugs. Growing up she would always be herself; she never tried to be like anyone else. She never went along with the crowd, and was never rowdy or loud. She has always followed her own mind, and thought for herself at all times. She is very dedicated to her job; will try to stick it out if it gets too hard. She is respectful to those of age; she choose her words carefully when she engage. She can also be stubborn at times, and refuse to give in to your point of mind. I give God the praise because of the person she is; he allowed me to instill life lessons in her, to follow in order to live.

No Other Way

God tests our faith in many ways; as we go through this life, we will have many hard days. Just when you think it is safe to breathe again; Satan will come back with another attack on man. God is allowing Satan to bring us sorrow and pain, because so many seem to have forgotten that God forever reigns. Some put their faith in men instead of seeking God's deliverance in this world of sin. We need to realize that God is our only hope, in a world filled with sin and disease that's beyond our scope. God is commanding every man, woman, boy, and girl to bow down and pray; because without him; there is just no other way.

Uneasy

There are some people that I have found; makes me uncomfortable to be around. Every time they come through the door, this uneasy feeling surface even more. They are always friendly and kind, but still there is something about them tugging at my mind. I ask myself "is it just me? Or am I just to blind to see. I ask God to help me see this person in another light; whether it's me or them, because something is just not right.

Where Will You Spend Eternity

Life is about choices! You either choose to live right, or you choose to live wrong; God gave us free will, and a mind of our own. There will come a day when we will have to say; I am on the beast, or the Lord's side, we won't be able to run away and hide. If we give up God to serve the beast, we will end up in hell where the fire never cease. If we hold on to God and his divine plan; eternal life is his promise to man. The choices we make in this life determine the outcome in God's eye sight.

A Humble Heart

A humble heart is as a little child; not boastful and loud, but calm and mild. A humble heart thinks of others first; because we are not alone in this vast universe. A humble heart is patient and kind; will not rush, but take their time. A humble heart is honest and true; would not do anything to cause harm to you. A humble heart is loving and sympathetic to others' grief and pain, with no thought of themselves, or any personal gain. A humble heart will always forgive; by trying to live according to God's will.

My Call

I am passionate about my call, to spread the good news to one and all. Through my poetry I give honor to Christ, so that it will help change someone's life. Christ loved us so much, he was willing to die; we couldn't save ourselves, that's the reason why. In order for him to reconcile us, we must believe, and in him trust. My call is to let all know that God loves you no matter what you do. Just call on him, and he will forgive your sins; just open your heart and he will come in. We gain salvation through his name, if we believe he died and rose again. My passion, my call; what better way to praise God than to uplift him to all.

I Don't Know You

A true friend is hard to find; a trait that's so rare in this day and time. Gone are the days we stuck together like glue; playing together, and fighting for each other too. As time went past, it brought about a change; you stopped coming around, or even mentioning my name. I tried to reach out to you, but you were too busy to talk, and had other things to do. You hung with others you considered your friends, but time will tell all in the end. True friendship never ends; we should be there for each other through thick and thin.

Don't Fool Yourself

You may fool people, but you can't fool God; he knows the true intentions of your heart. You may smile in my face, and give me a warm embrace, but is your heart truly in the right place? Are you really trying to live right? Or are your actions done to please others' sight? Do you have a heart full of love and a thoughtful mind? To do what you can to help people of all kinds. Do not fool yourself and think that you will get by; you can't escape God's judgement even if you try.

Beyond The Sky

Beyond the sky is our home on high; where we will no longer have to cry. We cannot see it with the natural eye, but our spiritual mind tells us that God cannot lie. Beyond the sky is our home on high; we are not living for life alone; we are living to serve and praise God, so we can make it to that home. If we live to serve and praise him; life is worth living when our eyes grow dim. If we live just to please ourself; when we leave this world, what will we have left? If we have faith in our home beyond the sky; we will live for God and soon rejoice in our home on high.

God's Instrument

An instrument can do nothing by itself; but it can do all things with God's divine help. We are instruments through which God can use, to spread the gospel of his good news. In a world where so many have lost all hope; and begin to think that they can no longer cope; just give a word to let them know that they are not alone; God is there for them to call on. He is with us all the time, and he knows what's on our mind. Just tell him what your problem is about, he will not shout it out. He is just waiting on you, to ask for strength to make it through. We are all instruments of God; but we must be willing to do our part. We are not in this world all by ourself; he can use each of us to encourage someone else.

Through It All

The hope of salvation began with christ; when he came down to earth and gave up his life; then God raised him from the grave, so that whoever believes would be saved. Through it all, he bore the shame, and the ridicule brought to his name. Through it all he never sinned; when he was on earth and lived among men. Through it all he stood his ground, and did not let Satan back him down. Through it all in his human form, he preached the good news so that men could be reborn.

Only Human

Don't put all your trust in man; he just can't do what God can. Man could not die for you; he was unworthy to carry it through. Man cannot forgive your sins, or have a Heaven or hell to put you in. Man cannot take away your pain; he has no power in his name. Man can't give you peace of mind, but the peace God gives is of the spiritual kind. Man cannot save your soul, to be redeemed by God is more precious than gold.

No Excuse

There's nothing we can do without God's say so; he gives us the strength to get up and go. If we are willing and able to go to other places; surely we can go to church and give God some praises. There is no excuse that will suffice; unless you are sick, and not able to assemble with Christians alike. We draw strength from one another, and spiritual well being to face our troubles. When we leave the service, we are able to stand; until the next time we all meet again.

God Promised

I cling to the hope of your promise, oh Lord! You said you would never leave us, and in you I will put my trust. Guide me down the right path; instill in me that trouble doesn't always last. You promised you would be with me in sickness and health; good times and bad, also in death. I hold on to the promise that you will always be with me; you are the only one that can mold me into what you would have me to be. Give me the mind to seek your ways that are holy, so that one day I will be in the presence of you and your glory.

Speak The Truth

Speak the truth instead of lies; God's word should not be compromised. Stop telling people what they want to hear, for it is God you have to fear. Speak the word if it's not received; you have done your part, and God is pleased. The word will draw them closer to God, or drive them away; if they take heed they will stay. Speak the word and they will know; God requires true service in order to grow. God gives us all free will; we make the choice on how we want to live.

My Only Comfort

I think back on the days when I lost my loved ones; the hurt I felt just couldn't be undone. There was a hole where my heart should be; an empty space no one could see. No one could take away that pain; I had to put it in God's hand. I had to bare that pain alone, and lean on God to keep me strong. A sudden or unexpected loss can shake your faith, but I know that God doesn't make any mistakes.

When We All Get Together

Do not do what others do, but to thine own self be true. Do not fail to assemble yourself, by trying to be like someone else. If they decide to stay at home; they are missing the fellowship that helps them stay strong. When we all come together on one accord; our praise goes up unto the Lord. When we are in agreement as one; the spirit of the Lord will surely come. We gain strength and encouragement from each other; when we come together with our sisters and brothers. Assemble yourselves with the Christian band, and never let go of God's unchanging hand.

A Conquering Faith

Perfect love is only accomplished through Christ, because of that love he gave up his life. God's only begotten son was made flesh when he was born. He is the source of our strength and love, that he sends to us from above. If Godly love abides in you, it will be seen in the things you say and do. Be confident in his love for you, and your faith will bring you through. A conquering faith will help you overcome, because your victory has already been won.

Past Events

I can't go back into the past, but the memories of them will always last. I close my eyes and I can see; past events that used to be. My hands stretched out as if to touch; the person or thing I loved so much. The special places I used to go; the people there I got to know. Past events that were so divine; transports me back to another time. Long ago and far behind; past events cloud my mind.

Traveling

Going on a trip alone can be scary when it's the first time you have ever left home. As you wave good-bye to the ones you hold dear; there is a sense of excitement and fear. The fear of what you are leaving behind; the excitement for what you hope you will find. The fear of doing new things in other places; the excitement of meeting all types of people from different races. The excitement of experiencing new heights, as you travel the world in awe of all the sights.

Joy In Salvation

Don't allow Satan to steal your joy; don't succumb to his devious ploy. Do not let him sway your mind; or have you doubting God all the time. Satan knows that God's words are true, so he will do whatever he can to discourage you. There's joy in the salvation of the lord; don't allow Satan to bring you discord. Don't allow Satan to wreak havoc in your life; hold on to the promise of Jesus Christ. Don't let him rob you of the joy that gives you peace of mind; knowing that God is with you all the time. Hold on to that joy, the joy of your salvation when you first accepted the Lord.

White Rose

This white rose is a symbol that you are not here; but God gave me memories of you that I will always hold dear. You showed your love for your children in so many ways, by doing whatever you could for all your days. Sitting on the porch together all day long; talking and watching traffic until the sun was gone. Precious memories I will always share; of my mother that did her best with love and care.

I Can Relate

To all the families on this somber day; my heart goes out to you in every way. I feel your grief, and I know the pain of dealing with a loss on this earthly plain. I know it's hard, but God helps us to cope; he did it for me, so don't give up hope.Ask him in prayer to help you to stand; to get through another day; and just hold onto his hand. He makes no mistakes, and it was his will; put your trust in him, and he will wipe away your tears.

No Greater Power

Although your life may sometimes get hard; there is no power greater than God. All that any of us can do is lean on God to bring us through. Men can't take our pain away or give us life to see another day. Men can't predict when we live or die, or why sometimes we have to cry. Men can only wonder what's going on in our life; but God has all power and knows our every strife. We all must live according to God's command; he is the only one who holds our souls in his hand.

A Praise In Your Heart

Always keep a praise in your heart, for he is a mighty and merciful God. Praise him for Jesus the son; the only one through whom our victory is won. Praise him for the stars at night; that light up the heavens and sparkle so bright. Praise him for the moon at night; praise him for the sun that gives off it's light. Praise him for the trees; that provide oxygen for us to breathe. Praise him for sending rain that helps plants, crops, and grass to grow; Praise him for the animals and insects also. Praise him when life begins to get hard; he is always there and will never depart. Praise him for the big things as well as the small; praise him for yourself, as well as for all. Praise him for the love he has for us; by creating each of us from the dust. Always keep a praise in your heart; for all things are possible, only through God.

www.ingramcontent.com/pod-product-compliance
Lightning Source LLC
LaVergne TN
LVHW091549060526
838200LV00036B/766